IFRS 15 Explained:

A Practical Handbook for Revenue Recognition

Mohd Arif

Preface

In the realm of financial accounting, revenue is often touted as the "top line" number, the initial figure that catches an investor's eye on an income statement. It is not merely a figure; it's a story of a company's transactions, a narration of its business activities, and a signpost of its market performance. With such significance attached to revenue, it is imperative that the method by which it's recognized and reported is both robust and reflective of economic reality.

The International Financial Reporting Standard (IFRS) 15, "Revenue from Contracts with Customers", introduced a new era for revenue recognition. Born out of a need to streamline varied practices and to instill greater transparency, IFRS 15 is comprehensive, universally applicable, and centered around a principle-based approach.

"IFRS 15 Explained: A Practical Handbook for Revenue Recognition" is an endeavor to bridge the understanding gap between the written standard and its real-world application. It is not just a retelling of the standard, but a practical guide enriched with case studies, scenarios, and solutions, crafted for professionals, students, and anyone in between. This book aims to elucidate the intricacies of IFRS 15, break down its complexities, and offer readers a clear path to navigate its requirements.

Within these pages, you'll find:

- A step-by-step exploration of the renowned five-step model.

- Real-world examples that span various industries and business models.

- A comprehensive look at disclosure requirements, complemented with practical examples.

- Common challenges faced during IFRS 15's implementation and solutions to overcome them.

- A dedicated section addressing frequently asked questions, demystifying common misconceptions.

While we have strived for clarity and thoroughness, the world of accounting standards is ever-evolving. Readers are encouraged to consult the original IFRS publications, engage in continuous professional development, and always seek expert advice when faced with intricate scenarios.

In closing, I hope this book serves as a valuable companion in your journey through IFRS 15. Whether you are a seasoned professional, an accounting student, or merely an enthusiast seeking clarity, may these pages provide the insights you seek.

Happy reading and onward to a clearer understanding of revenue recognition in today's dynamic business landscape.

Mohd Arif

Index

Chapter 1: Introduction

What is IFRS 15?

The International Financial Reporting Standards (IFRS), governed by the International Accounting Standards Board (IASB), form the cornerstone of financial reporting standards across many countries globally. IFRS aims to bring about consistency, transparency, and comparability in financial statements, enabling stakeholders from diverse geographies to interpret financial data with uniformity.

Among these standards, IFRS 15, titled "Revenue from Contracts with Customers", holds a special significance. Introduced to replace a slew of previous revenue-related standards and interpretations, IFRS 15 offers a comprehensive framework on how entities should recognize revenue from contracts with customers.

At its core, IFRS 15 aims to achieve two primary objectives:

1. To create a robust and cohesive framework for revenue recognition, eliminating the boundaries of industry-specific requirements and providing a single, universally applicable standard.

2. To enhance the clarity and detail of revenue-related disclosures, aiding stakeholders in understanding the nature, amount, timing, and uncertainties of revenue and cash flows from contracts with customers.

The Importance of Revenue Recognition in Financial Reporting

Revenue recognition is one of the most pivotal concepts in financial accounting. Its significance extends beyond the mere presentation of a number on the income statement. Proper revenue recognition provides valuable insights into the financial health, performance, and future prospects of an entity. Here's an in-depth exploration of its importance:

1. **Mirror to Economic Activities**: Revenue recognition that aligns with a company's economic activities provides a transparent mirror to its operations. When revenue is recognized appropriately, it captures the essence of a company's transactions, accurately reflecting its dealings with customers, suppliers, and other stakeholders.

2. **Basis for Decision-making**: For investors, creditors, and other external stakeholders, revenue is often a starting point for analysis. Decisions regarding investments, lending, and credit are, in many instances, based on how well a company can generate revenue. Misleading revenue figures can result in misguided and potentially detrimental decisions.

3. **Comparability Across Companies**: In the era of globalization, investors and stakeholders often look across borders for investment opportunities. A consistent approach to revenue recognition, as seen with IFRS 15, ensures that businesses from diverse geographies and sectors can be compared on an equal footing.

4. **Forecasting & Predictability**: Properly recognized revenue allows stakeholders to predict future revenue streams, especially in businesses with recurring revenue models. This forward-looking approach is crucial for strategies concerning expansion, investment, and market entry.

5. **Integrity & Credibility**: Inconsistent or manipulated revenue figures can erode trust. Adhering to established revenue recognition principles enhances the credibility of financial statements, fostering trust among investors, regulators, and the broader market.

6. **Operational Insights**: Beyond external stakeholders, accurate revenue recognition offers valuable insights for management. It can indicate the success of product launches, effectiveness of marketing campaigns, seasonal fluctuations in demand, and more.

7. **Regulatory and Tax Implications**: Governments and regulatory bodies often use revenue figures for taxation and compliance purposes. Accurate recognition ensures that businesses meet their legal obligations, reducing risks associated with non-compliance.

8. **Stakeholder Confidence**: Stakeholders, including shareholders, employees, and customers, derive confidence from a company's financial performance. Reliable revenue figures can boost morale, improve stock prices, and enhance customer trust.

9. **Linkage to Performance Metrics**: Many companies have performance metrics and bonuses tied to revenue targets. Proper recognition ensures that these metrics are meaningful and that rewards align with genuine achievements.

In summary, revenue recognition is not just an accounting formality; it's a fundamental practice that impacts a wide range of stakeholders and a multitude of business decisions. As financial markets evolve and become more interconnected, the significance of robust, transparent, and consistent revenue recognition practices will only amplify.

Chapter 2: The Core Principles of IFRS 15

Introduction to the Core Principles

IFRS 15, "Revenue from Contracts with Customers," was established to provide entities with clear and comprehensive guidelines for recognizing revenue in a consistent and meaningful manner across industries and geographies. At the heart of this standard lie its core principles, designed to ensure that revenue recognition reflects the true economic nature of the underlying transactions.

Objective of IFRS 15

The main objective of IFRS 15 is to provide a framework that ensures that entities recognize revenue in a manner that depicts the transfer of promised goods or services to customers, in an amount reflecting the consideration to which the entity expects to be entitled in exchange for those goods or services.

The Five Core Principles

1. **Identify the Contract with a Customer:**

    - A contract is defined as an agreement between parties creating enforceable rights and obligations.

    - The criteria include the approval and commitment of both parties, the identification of each party's rights, payment terms, and the likelihood of the entity receiving the promised consideration.

2. **Identify the Performance Obligations in the Contract:**

    - A performance obligation is a promise to transfer goods or services to a customer.

    - The principle requires an entity to identify all individual performance obligations, which can be distinct goods or services or a series of distinct goods or services that are substantially the same.

3. **Determine the Transaction Price**:

- This is the amount of consideration an entity expects to receive in exchange for transferring goods or services.

- Factors such as variable consideration, significant financing components, non-cash consideration, and consideration payable to the customer are taken into account.

4. **Allocate the Transaction Price to the Performance Obligations**:

- Once the transaction price is determined, the next step is to allocate that price to individual performance obligations based on standalone selling prices.

- This ensures that the revenue recognized for each obligation accurately mirrors the value delivered to the customer.

5. **Recognize Revenue when (or as) the Entity Satisfies a Performance Obligation**:

- Revenue is recognized when the customer gains control of the promised good or service, either over time or at a point in time.

- This principle ensures that revenue matches the actual transfer of value to the customer.

Conclusion

The core principles of IFRS 15 provide a systematic and structured approach to revenue recognition. By adhering to these principles, entities can ensure that their financial statements offer a transparent, accurate, and comparable depiction of their revenue-generating activities. As we delve deeper into subsequent chapters, we'll explore the practical application of each of these principles, providing readers with tangible insights into the real-world implications of IFRS 15.

Chapter 3: The Five-Step Model Explained

The Five-Step Model forms the backbone of IFRS 15, "Revenue from Contracts with Customers." Serving as a structured guideline, this model aids entities in determining when and how much revenue should be recognized. Let's embark on a detailed journey through each of these steps.

Step 1: Identify the Contract with a Customer

- **Definition**: A contract is an agreement that creates enforceable rights and obligations.

- **Criteria for a Contract**:

    - Both parties have approved the agreement.

    - Each party's rights regarding goods or services are identified.

    - Payment terms are specified.

    - The entity expects to collect the consideration for which it is entitled.

- **Considerations**: Companies must regularly review contracts to ascertain if they meet the criteria, especially if circumstances change.

Step 2: Identify the Performance Obligations in the Contract

- **Definition**: A performance obligation is a promise in a contract to transfer a distinct good or service to the customer.

- **Distinct Goods or Services**:

    - The customer can benefit from the good or service on its own or in conjunction with other readily available resources.

    - The promise to transfer the good or service is distinct within the context of the contract.

- **Bundling**: If multiple goods or services are bundled in a contract and are not distinct, they are treated as a single performance obligation.

Step 3: Determine the Transaction Price

- **Definition**: The transaction price is the amount the entity expects to receive in exchange for transferring the promised goods or services.

- **Variables and Adjustments**:

    - Consider variable considerations such as discounts, rebates, and bonuses.

    - Adjust for the time value of money if there is a significant financing component.

    - Non-cash considerations should be measured at fair value.

    - Consider any amounts payable to the customer.

Step 4: Allocate the Transaction Price to the Performance Obligations

- **Basis**: Allocation is generally based on the standalone selling price (SSP) of each distinct good or service.

- **Estimating SSP**: If the standalone selling price isn't directly observable, entities must estimate it, considering market conditions, competitor actions, and any internal factors.

- **Discounts and Variable Considerations**: Allocate discounts and any variable consideration to all performance obligations unless specific criteria are met for allocation to one or more distinct obligations.

Step 5: Recognize Revenue when (or as) the Entity Satisfies a Performance Obligation

- **Point in Time vs. Over Time**: Determine if the revenue recognition occurs at a single point in time or over a period.

    - *Over Time*: If the customer simultaneously receives and consumes the benefits, if the entity's performance creates or enhances an asset, or if the entity's performance does not create an asset with an alternative use and the entity has an enforceable right to payment.

    - *Point in Time*: If none of the 'over time' criteria are met.

- **Considerations**: Entities must evaluate the customer's control (not possession) over the asset, considering if they have the ability to direct its use and benefit from it.

In Conclusion

The Five-Step Model of IFRS 15 may initially appear complex, but its structured approach brings clarity and consistency to the revenue recognition process. With its focus on contracts and performance obligations, the model ensures that revenue is recognized in a manner that mirrors the delivery of value to the customer. As we proceed, we'll dive into real-life examples and scenarios that illuminate the application of this model in various business contexts.

Chapter 4: Practical Scenarios & Case Studies

Navigating through IFRS 15's theoretical underpinnings is one task; applying it in real-world scenarios is another. In this chapter, we'll present practical scenarios and case studies across various industries to demonstrate the application and intricacies of the Five-Step Model.

Scenario 1: Software Company - Multi-Component Sales

Background: A software company sells a bundled package that includes software licenses, post-contract customer support, and periodic software updates.

Application:

1. **Identify the Contract**: The company enters into a contract with the customer for a one-year bundled package.

2. **Identify Performance Obligations**: The contract has three distinct obligations:

   - Software license

   - Customer support

   - Software updates

3. **Determine Transaction Price**: The bundled price is $1,200.

4. **Allocate Transaction Price**: Assuming standalone prices are $900 for the license, $200 for support, and $100 for updates, the transaction price is allocated proportionally.

5. **Recognize Revenue**:

   - License: Recognized at the point of sale ($900).

   - Support: Recognized evenly over the year ($16.67/month).

   - Updates: Recognized as updates are provided.

Scenario 2: Construction Company - Over Time Recognition

Background: A construction company has a two-year contract to build a bridge.

Application:

1. **Identify the Contract**: A two-year contract to construct a bridge.

2. **Identify Performance Obligations**: The primary obligation is to deliver a fully constructed bridge.

3. **Determine Transaction Price**: The contract price is $10 million.

4. **Allocate Transaction Price**: The entire amount is allocated to the single performance obligation.

5. **Recognize Revenue**:

   - Recognized over time based on the progress towards completion. If, after the first year, 60% of the work is completed, $6 million (60% of $10 million) is recognized in the first year.

Scenario 3: Publishing House - Variable Consideration

Background: A publishing house signs a contract with an author for a book. The author receives an advance, and further payments are contingent upon sales milestones.

Application:

1. **Identify the Contract**: Agreement with the author for publishing and selling the book.

2. **Identify Performance Obligations**: The obligation is to publish and distribute the book.

3. **Determine Transaction Price**: The advance is $50,000. Further payments, based on sales, are estimated to be $30,000, but they might vary.

4. **Allocate Transaction Price**: The initial transaction price is the advance, with future amounts adjusted based on actual sales milestones.

5. **Recognize Revenue**:

   - The advance is recognized as a liability initially.

   - As books are sold, revenue is recognized, and the liability (advance) is reduced. Additional revenue is recognized as sales milestones are achieved.

Scenario 4: Telecom Operator - Bundled Services

Background: A telecom company offers a bundled package with a mobile handset, voice plan, and data plan.

Application:

1. **Identify the Contract**: A two-year bundled service agreement.

2. **Identify Performance Obligations**:

- Handset

- Monthly voice services

- Monthly data services

3. **Determine Transaction Price**: The bundled price is $1,000.

4. **Allocate Transaction Price**: Estimated standalone prices are $400 for the handset, $300 for voice services, and $300 for data services. Allocation is proportional.

5. **Recognize Revenue**:

   - Handset: Recognized immediately ($400).

   - Voice and Data: Recognized monthly over two years ($12.50/month for each service).

Scenario 5: Automobile Dealership - Free Maintenance

Background: An auto dealership sells a car with a one-year free maintenance service.

Application:

1. **Identify the Contract**: Sale of a car with an added one-year maintenance service.

2. **Identify Performance Obligations**: Two distinct obligations:

   - Car

   - Maintenance service

3. **Determine Transaction Price**: Sale price is $20,000, inclusive of maintenance.

4. **Allocate Transaction Price**: If the standalone price of the maintenance service is $1,200, allocate proportionally.

5. **Recognize Revenue**:

- Car: Immediately ($18,800).

- Maintenance: Recognized over the year ($100/month).

Scenario 6: Subscription Box Service

Background: A company offers monthly beauty subscription boxes containing various products.

Application:

1. **Identify the Contract**: Monthly subscription for a beauty box.

2. **Identify Performance Obligations**: Delivering the beauty box every month.

3. **Determine Transaction Price**: Monthly subscription fee of $30.

4. **Allocate Transaction Price**: Entire amount is for the beauty box.

5. **Recognize Revenue**: As each box is delivered monthly.

Scenario 7: Movie Production House - Licensing Agreement

Background: A movie house licenses its movies to a streaming platform for a fixed period.

Application:

1. **Identify the Contract**: Licensing of movies for streaming.

2. **Identify Performance Obligations**: Granting access to the movies for a specified period.

3. **Determine Transaction Price**: Licensing fee of $2 million for 2 years.

4. **Allocate Transaction Price**: Entire fee allocated to the licensing right.

5. **Recognize Revenue**: Recognized over the 2-year period ($83,333/month).

Scenario 8: Real Estate - Sale of Apartments

Background: A real estate developer sells apartments, and buyers can move in only after full payment.

Application:

1. **Identify the Contract**: Sale of an apartment.

2. **Identify Performance Obligations**: Delivering the possession of the apartment.

3. **Determine Transaction Price**: Selling price is $200,000.

4. **Allocate Transaction Price**: Entire amount for the apartment.

5. **Recognize Revenue**: Once full payment is received and possession is given.

Scenario 9: Online Course Platform - Lifetime Access

Background: An e-learning platform sells courses with lifetime access.

Application:

1. **Identify the Contract**: Sale of an online course with lifetime access.

2. **Identify Performance Obligations**: Granting access to course materials indefinitely.

3. **Determine Transaction Price**: Course fee is $500.

4. **Allocate Transaction Price**: Entire amount for course access.

5. **Recognize Revenue**: Recognized immediately upon sale.

Scenario 10: Fitness Center - Annual Membership with Personal Training

Background: A fitness center sells an annual membership and offers 10 personal training sessions.

Application:

1. **Identify the Contract**: One-year gym membership with personal training sessions.

2. **Identify Performance Obligations**:

    - Access to gym facilities.

    - Personal training sessions.

3. **Determine Transaction Price**: Combined price is $1,200.

4. **Allocate Transaction Price**: If standalone prices are $1,000 for membership and $200 for training, allocate proportionally.

5. **Recognize Revenue**:

    - Membership: Over the year ($83.33/month).

    - Training: As each session is provided.

Scenario 11: Airline Company - Loyalty Points

Background: An airline gives loyalty points for each flight, redeemable for future travel or upgrades.

Application:

1. **Identify the Contract**: Flight service with loyalty points as a bonus.

2. **Identify Performance Obligations**:

- Flight service.

- Future services/upgrades via loyalty points.

3. **Determine Transaction Price**: If a ticket costs $300 and points given can get services worth $30.

4. **Allocate Transaction Price**: Allocate $270 to flight and $30 to loyalty points.

5. **Recognize Revenue**:

- Flight: Immediately.

- Loyalty Points: When redeemed by the customer.

Scenario 12: Concert Organizer - VIP Packages

Background: An organizer sells VIP packages including concert tickets, backstage access, and merchandise.

Application:

1. **Identify the Contract**: Sale of a VIP concert package.

2. **Identify Performance Obligations**:

- Concert access.

- Backstage pass.

- Merchandise.

3. **Determine Transaction Price**: VIP package price is $500.

4. **Allocate Transaction Price**: If standalone prices are $300 for ticket, $150 for backstage access, and $50 for merchandise, allocate proportionally.

5. **Recognize Revenue**:

- Ticket and Backstage: On the concert day.

- Merchandise: When handed over to the customer.

Scenario 13: Magazine Publisher - Annual Subscription with Free Book

Background: A publisher offers an annual magazine subscription and gives a free book as an incentive.

Application:

1. **Identify the Contract**: Annual magazine subscription with a free book.

2. **Identify Performance Obligations**:

   - Monthly magazine delivery.

   - Free book.

3. **Determine Transaction Price**: Subscription fee is $120.

4. **Allocate Transaction Price**: If the estimated standalone price of the book is $20, allocate $100 to the subscription and $20 to the book.

5. **Recognize Revenue**:

   - Magazine: Monthly as each issue is delivered ($8.33/month).

   - Book: When it's delivered to the subscriber.

Scenario 14: Consulting Firm - Milestone Payments

Background: A consulting firm offers services with payments tied to project milestones.

Application:

1. **Identify the Contract**: Consulting project with milestones.

2. **Identify Performance Obligations**: Deliverables at each milestone.

3. **Determine Transaction Price**: Total fee is $50,000, with payments at various milestones.

4. **Allocate Transaction Price**: Proportional to the value provided at each milestone.

5. **Recognize Revenue**: As each milestone is achieved and approved by the client.

Scenario 15: Mobile Game Developer - In-App Purchases

Background: A game developer offers in-app purchases, including virtual goods and power-ups.

Application:

1. **Identify the Contract**: Purchase within the game application.

2. **Identify Performance Obligations**: Delivery of virtual goods or power-ups.

3. **Determine Transaction Price**: Price varies based on the in-app item purchased.

4. **Allocate Transaction Price**: Entire amount to the respective virtual item.

5. **Recognize Revenue**: Immediately upon confirmation of the in-app purchase.

Scenario 16: Catering Service - Advance Bookings

Background: A catering company takes bookings for future events, with a partial advance.

Application:

1. **Identify the Contract**: Catering service for a future event.

2. **Identify Performance Obligations**: Providing food and service at the event.

3. **Determine Transaction Price**: Total cost is $5,000, with a $1,000 advance.

4. **Allocate Transaction Price**: Entire amount to the catering service.

5. **Recognize Revenue**: After the event, when the service has been rendered.

Scenario 17: Renewable Energy Company - Installation and Service

Background: A company sells solar panels with installation and a two-year service plan.

Application:

1. **Identify the Contract**: Sale and installation of solar panels with a service plan.

2. **Identify Performance Obligations**:

   - Solar panels.

   - Installation.

   - Two-year service.

3. **Determine Transaction Price**: Combined price is $10,000.

4. **Allocate Transaction Price**: If standalone prices are $7,000 for panels, $2,000 for installation, and $1,000 for service, allocate proportionally.

5. **Recognize Revenue**:

   - Panels and Installation: Once installed.

   - Service: Over the two-year period ($41.67/month).

Scenario 18: Home Security Company - Hardware and Monthly Monitoring

Background: A company sells security hardware and offers a monthly monitoring service.

Application:

1. **Identify the Contract**: Sale of security equipment with monthly monitoring.

2. **Identify Performance Obligations**:

   - Security hardware.

   - Monthly monitoring.

3. **Determine Transaction Price**: One-time hardware cost of $1,000 and a monthly fee of $50 for monitoring.

4. **Allocate Transaction Price**: Entire hardware cost to the equipment and the monthly fee to monitoring.

5. **Recognize Revenue**:

   - Hardware: Immediately upon installation.

   - Monitoring: Monthly, as the service is provided.

Background: A fashion brand allows customers to pre-order items before they are released.

Application:

1. **Identify the Contract**: Pre-order of a fashion item.

2. **Identify Performance Obligations**: Delivering the pre-ordered item.

3. **Determine Transaction Price**: Price is $200 for the pre-ordered item.

4. **Allocate Transaction Price**: Entire amount to the fashion item.

5. **Recognize Revenue**: Once the item is shipped or made available to the customer.

Scenario 20: Hotel Chain - Loyalty Program

Background: A hotel chain offers loyalty points for each stay, which can be redeemed for future stays or other benefits.

Application:

1. **Identify the Contract**: Hotel stay with loyalty points granted.

2. **Identify Performance Obligations**:

   - Hotel stay.

   - Future stays or benefits via loyalty points.

3. **Determine Transaction Price**: If a room costs $150 and points given equate to benefits worth $15.

4. **Allocate Transaction Price**: Allocate $135 to the room stay and $15 to the loyalty points.

5. **Recognize Revenue**:

- Room Stay: Immediately.

- Loyalty Points: When redeemed by the guest.

Scenario 21: Telecommunications - Bundled Contracts

Background: A telecom company offers a bundled package of a smartphone and a two-year service contract.

Application:

1. **Identify the Contract**: Sale of smartphone with a two-year service contract.

2. **Identify Performance Obligations**:

   - Smartphone.

   - Two-year service contract.

3. **Determine Transaction Price**: Combined price is $1,200.

4. **Allocate Transaction Price**: If standalone prices are $800 for the phone and $400 for the service, allocate proportionally.

5. **Recognize Revenue**:

   - Smartphone: Immediately.

   - Service: Over the two-year period.

Scenario 22: Publishing - Multi-volume Set

Background: A publisher sells a 5-volume book series, shipped as each book is released.

Application:

1. **Identify the Contract**: Sale of a 5-volume series.

2. **Identify Performance Obligations**: Each book in the series.

3. **Determine Transaction Price**: Series price is $100.

4. **Allocate Transaction Price**: $20 per book.

5. **Recognize Revenue**: As each volume is shipped.

Scenario 23: Software - Perpetual License with Support

Background: A software company sells software with a perpetual license and a one-year support.

Application:

1. **Identify the Contract**: Software sale with a support contract.

2. **Identify Performance Obligations**:

   - Software license.

   - One-year support.

3. **Determine Transaction Price**: Combined price is $2,000.

4. **Allocate Transaction Price**: If standalone prices are $1,500 for the license and $500 for the support, allocate proportionally.

5. **Recognize Revenue**:

   - Software License: Immediately.

   - Support: Over the one-year period.

Scenario 24: Agriculture - Crop Shares

Background: A farmer enters a contract where he provides land and another party plants and harvests, splitting the produce.

Application:

1. **Identify the Contract**: Crop sharing agreement.

2. **Identify Performance Obligations**: Sharing the produce at harvest.

3. **Determine Transaction Price**: Not monetary but based on percentage split of produce.

4. **Allocate Transaction Price**: Based on the agreed percentage.

5. **Recognize Revenue**: At harvest when produce is shared.

Scenario 25: SaaS (Software as a Service) Platform

Background: A company offers a monthly subscription to its online software platform.

Application:

1. **Identify the Contract**: Monthly software subscription.

2. **Identify Performance Obligations**: Monthly access to the software platform.

3. **Determine Transaction Price**: Monthly subscription fee of $30.

4. **Allocate Transaction Price**: Entire amount for monthly access.

5. **Recognize Revenue**: Each month as access is provided.

Scenario 26: Travel Agency - All-Inclusive Packages

Background: A travel agency offers packages including flights, hotel stays, and excursions.

Application:

1. **Identify the Contract**: All-inclusive travel package.

2. **Identify Performance Obligations**:

- Flight.

- Hotel stay.

- Excursions.

3. **Determine Transaction Price**: Combined package price of $2,500.

4. **Allocate Transaction Price**: Based on estimated standalone selling prices.

5. **Recognize Revenue**:

   - Flight: When taken.

   - Hotel Stay: Over the duration of the stay.

   - Excursions: When they occur.

Scenario 27: Art Gallery - Artwork on Consignment

Background: An artist provides artwork to a gallery on consignment.

Application:

1. **Identify the Contract**: Artwork consignment agreement.

2. **Identify Performance Obligations**: Sale of artwork.

3. **Determine Transaction Price**: Price is agreed upon beforehand or determined upon sale.

4. **Allocate Transaction Price**: Entire amount to the artwork.

5. **Recognize Revenue**: Once the artwork is sold.

Scenario 28: Healthcare - Medical Procedures with Payment Plans

Background: A hospital provides medical procedures and allows patients to pay in installments.

Application:

1. **Identify the Contract**: Medical procedure with a payment plan.

2. **Identify Performance Obligations**: Medical procedure.

3. **Determine Transaction Price**: Total price of the procedure, regardless of payment plan.

4. **Allocate Transaction Price**: Entire amount to the procedure.

5. **Recognize Revenue**: When the procedure is performed.

Scenario 29: Construction - Progress Billing

Background: A construction company has a contract to build a shopping mall, with progress billings.

Application:

1. **Identify the Contract**: Mall construction contract.

2. **Identify Performance Obligations**: Completion of the shopping mall.

3. **Determine Transaction Price**: Agreed upon price in contract.

4. **Allocate Transaction Price**: Based on progress milestones.

5. **Recognize Revenue**: As each milestone is achieved.

Scenario 30: Online Marketplace - Sale of Goods by Third Parties

Background: An online platform allows third parties to sell goods, taking a commission.

Application:

1. **Identify the Contract**: Agreement between the platform and third-party sellers.

2. **Identify Performance Obligations**: Facilitating the sale.

3. **Determine Transaction Price**: Commission on each sale.

4. **Allocate Transaction Price**: Entire commission to the platform.

5. **Recognize Revenue**: Upon the sale of goods by the third party.

Scenario 31: Insurance - Multi-year Policy

Background: An insurance company sells a five-year life insurance policy.

Application:

1. **Identify the Contract**: Five-year life insurance policy.

2. **Identify Performance Obligations**: Coverage over the five years.

3. **Determine Transaction Price**: Premium for the five-year policy.

4. **Allocate Transaction Price**: Pro-rata over the five years.

5. **Recognize Revenue**: Annually over the five-year period.

Scenario 32: Broadcasting - Advertisement Slots

Background: A TV station sells advertisement slots during prime time.

Application:

1. **Identify the Contract**: Sale of advertisement slots.

2. **Identify Performance Obligations**: Airing the advertisement during the specified time.

3. **Determine Transaction Price**: Price for the ad slot.

4. **Allocate Transaction Price**: Entire amount to the ad slot.

5. **Recognize Revenue**: Once the advertisement is aired.

Scenario 33: Research & Development - Milestone Payments

Background: A biotech firm is paid to develop a new drug, with milestone payments.

Application:

1. **Identify the Contract**: Drug development contract.

2. **Identify Performance Obligations**: Achieving specific development milestones.

3. **Determine Transaction Price**: Payments for each milestone.

4. **Allocate Transaction Price**: To each respective milestone.

5. **Recognize Revenue**: Upon achieving each milestone.

Scenario 34: Subscription Box Service

Background: A company offers a monthly subscription box with curated goods.

Application:

1. **Identify the Contract**: Monthly subscription box service.

2. **Identify Performance Obligations**: Monthly delivery of curated goods.

3. **Determine Transaction Price**: Monthly fee.

4. **Allocate Transaction Price**: Entire amount to the monthly box.

5. **Recognize Revenue**: Each month when the box is shipped.

Scenario 35: Music Artist - Royalties from Streaming

Background: A musician receives royalties for their music being streamed online.

Application:

1. **Identify the Contract**: Agreement with streaming service.

2. **Identify Performance Obligations**: Availability of music for streaming.

3. **Determine Transaction Price**: Royalties based on streaming counts.

4. **Allocate Transaction Price**: Based on respective song or album streams.

5. **Recognize Revenue**: As the music is streamed.

Scenario 36: Licensing - Brand Name on Apparel

Background: A famous brand licenses its name to an apparel manufacturer.

Application:

1. **Identify the Contract**: Licensing agreement.

2. **Identify Performance Obligations**: Use of brand name on apparel.

3. **Determine Transaction Price**: Licensing fee or royalty.

4. **Allocate Transaction Price**: Based on sales or a flat fee.

5. **Recognize Revenue**: As apparel is sold or based on the agreement terms.

Scenario 37: Professional Training - Workshops & Materials

Background: A training organization offers workshops and provides materials.

Application:

1. **Identify the Contract**: Workshop enrollment.

2. **Identify Performance Obligations**:

    - Workshop delivery.

    - Materials provided.

3. **Determine Transaction Price**: Combined price for workshop and materials.

4. **Allocate Transaction Price**: Based on estimated standalone selling prices.

5. **Recognize Revenue**:

    - Workshop: When conducted.

    - Materials: When provided.

Scenario 38: Real Estate - Property Sale with Future Upgrades

Background: A property developer sells properties with a promise of future amenities.

Application:

1. **Identify the Contract**: Sale of property with future amenities.

2. **Identify Performance Obligations**:

   - Property sale.

   - Future amenities.

3. **Determine Transaction Price**: Combined price for property and promised amenities.

4. **Allocate Transaction Price**: Based on estimated standalone selling prices.

5. **Recognize Revenue**:

   - Property: Upon sale.

   - Amenities: As they are developed.

Scenario 39: Gym Membership - Free Personal Training Sessions

Background: A gym offers a membership package that includes free personal training sessions.

Application:

1. **Identify the Contract**: Gym membership with personal training.

2. **Identify Performance Obligations**:

   - Gym access.

- Personal training sessions.

3. **Determine Transaction Price**: Combined membership fee.

4. **Allocate Transaction Price**: Based on estimated standalone selling prices.

5. **Recognize Revenue**:

   - Gym access: Monthly.

   - Training sessions: As they occur.

Scenario 40: Film Production - Sale to Streaming Service

Background: A film production company sells rights to a film to a streaming service.

Application:

1. **Identify the Contract**: Film rights sale.

2. **Identify Performance Obligations**: Providing the film for streaming.

3. **Determine Transaction Price**: Agreed sale price for the film rights.

4. **Allocate Transaction Price**: Entire amount to the film rights.

5. **Recognize Revenue**: Upon transfer of rights to the streaming service.

Scenario 41: Web Development - Website with Monthly Maintenance

Background: A web developer creates a website for a client and offers monthly maintenance.

Application:

1. **Identify the Contract**: Web development and maintenance contract.

2. **Identify Performance Obligations**:

   - Website creation.

   - Monthly maintenance.

3. **Determine Transaction Price**: Combined fee for website creation and maintenance.

4. **Allocate Transaction Price**: Based on estimated standalone selling prices.

5. **Recognize Revenue**:

   - Website: Upon completion.

   - Maintenance: Monthly.

Scenario 42: Aircraft Manufacturer - Plane Sale with Pilot Training

Background: An aircraft manufacturer sells planes and provides pilot training.

Application:

1. **Identify the Contract**: Sale of aircraft with pilot training.

2. **Identify Performance Obligations**:

   - Aircraft delivery.

   - Pilot training.

3. **Determine Transaction Price**: Combined price for aircraft and training.

4. **Allocate Transaction Price**: Based on estimated standalone selling prices.

5. **Recognize Revenue**:

    - Aircraft: Upon delivery.

    - Training: When conducted.

Scenario 43: Jewelry Store - Custom Orders

Background: A jewelry store creates custom pieces based on customer specifications.

Application:

1. **Identify the Contract**: Custom jewelry order.

2. **Identify Performance Obligations**: Creation and delivery of the custom piece.

3. **Determine Transaction Price**: Agreed price for the custom order.

4. **Allocate Transaction Price**: Entire amount to the custom order.

5. **Recognize Revenue**: Upon completion and delivery.

Scenario 44: Transportation - Multi-leg Journey

Background: A transport company offers a multi-leg journey (e.g., bus to train transfer).

Application:

1. **Identify the Contract**: Multi-leg transportation ticket.

2. **Identify Performance Obligations**:

    - Bus segment.

- Train segment.

3. **Determine Transaction Price**: Combined ticket price.

4. **Allocate Transaction Price**: Based on estimated standalone ticket prices.

5. **Recognize Revenue**:

   - Bus: After bus journey.

   - Train: After train journey.

Scenario 45: Online Education - Course with Certification

Background: An online platform offers courses that come with certification upon completion.

Application:

1. **Identify the Contract**: Online course with certification.

2. **Identify Performance Obligations**:

   - Course access.

   - Certification.

3. **Determine Transaction Price**: Combined course fee.

4. **Allocate Transaction Price**: Based on estimated standalone selling prices.

5. **Recognize Revenue**:

   - Course: As it's accessed.

   - Certification: Once issued.

Scenario 46: Cleaning Service - Regular Cleaning with Annual Deep Clean

Background: A cleaning company offers a package of regular cleaning and an annual deep clean.

Application:

1. **Identify the Contract**: Cleaning package.

2. **Identify Performance Obligations**:

   - Regular cleaning.

   - Annual deep clean.

3. **Determine Transaction Price**: Combined package price.

4. **Allocate Transaction Price**: Based on estimated standalone selling prices.

5. **Recognize Revenue**:

   - Regular cleaning: As services are rendered.

   - Deep clean: Once annually when performed.

Scenario 47: Video Game Developer - Game with Future DLCs

Background: A developer releases a game with promises of future downloadable content (DLC).

Application:

1. **Identify the Contract**: Game sale with future DLCs.

2. **Identify Performance Obligations**:

   - Game sale.

   - Future DLCs.

3. **Determine Transaction Price**: Price for the game with future DLCs.

4. **Allocate Transaction Price**: Based on estimated standalone selling prices.

5. **Recognize Revenue**:

    - Game: Upon sale.

    - DLCs: As they're released.

Scenario 48: Catering - Event Catering with Follow-up Services

Background: A catering company provides food for an event and offers follow-up services like cleaning.

Application:

1. **Identify the Contract**: Catering for event with follow-up services.

2. **Identify Performance Obligations**:

    - Food catering.

    - Cleaning services.

3. **Determine Transaction Price**: Combined fee for catering and cleaning.

4. **Allocate Transaction Price**: Based on estimated standalone selling prices.

5. **Recognize Revenue**:

    - Catering: After the event.

    - Cleaning: Once completed.

Scenario 49: Car Dealership - Sale with Extended Warranty

Background: A car dealership sells cars and offers extended warranties.

Application:

1. **Identify the Contract**: Car sale with extended warranty.

2. **Identify Performance Obligations**:

   - Car sale.

   - Extended warranty.

3. **Determine Transaction Price**: Combined car price and warranty fee.

4. **Allocate Transaction Price**: Based on estimated standalone selling prices.

5. **Recognize Revenue**:

   - Car: Upon sale.

   - Warranty: Over the warranty period.

Scenario 50: Architecture Firm - Design with On-site Supervision

Background: An architecture firm designs a building and provides on-site supervision during construction.

Application:

1. **Identify the Contract**: Architectural design with supervision.

2. **Identify Performance Obligations**:

   - Design creation.

   - On-site supervision.

3. **Determine Transaction Price**: Combined fee for design and supervision.

4. **Allocate Transaction Price**: Based on estimated standalone selling prices.

5. **Recognize Revenue**:

   - Design: Once finalized.

   - Supervision: Over the construction period.

Complex contract arrangements often arise in industries where goods or services are intertwined, where multiple performance obligations exist, or where there's significant judgment involved in pricing, deliverability, or revenue recognition. Understanding and applying IFRS 15 to these contracts can be challenging. Let's delve into a few examples of complex contract arrangements:

1. Bundled Goods and Services

A telecommunications company might offer a contract that includes a mobile phone, a monthly service plan, and a music streaming subscription.

- **Challenge**: How to allocate the transaction price among these distinct goods and services?

Application:

1. **Identify the Contract**: Agreement with the customer.

2. **Identify Performance Obligations**: Mobile phone, monthly service plan, music subscription.

3. **Determine Transaction Price**: Total contract amount.

4. **Allocate Transaction Price**: Based on standalone selling prices of each component.

5. **Recognize Revenue**: As each obligation is satisfied.

2. Milestone-based Contracts in Research and Development

A pharmaceutical company enters into an agreement to develop a drug, with payments based on research milestones.

- **Challenge**: When should revenue be recognized given the uncertain nature of research outcomes?

Application:

1. **Identify the Contract**: Research and development agreement.

2. **Identify Performance Obligations**: Each research milestone.

3. **Determine Transaction Price**: Total potential amount, considering the probability of reaching each milestone.

4. **Allocate Transaction Price**: To each milestone based on its standalone value.

5. **Recognize Revenue**: As each milestone is achieved.

3. Real Estate Sales with Post-sale Services

A developer sells properties and promises post-sale services like community development or maintenance.

- **Challenge**: How to recognize revenue for post-sale services that span years?

Application:

1. **Identify the Contract**: Sale of property with post-sale services.

2. **Identify Performance Obligations**: Property sale, future community development, maintenance.

3. **Determine Transaction Price**: Combined property price and service fees.

4. **Allocate Transaction Price**: Based on standalone selling prices.

5. **Recognize Revenue**: Property upon sale, services over the period of provision.

4. Software Licensing with Post-contract Support

A software company sells a license with a promise of updates and support for the next three years.

- **Challenge**: When to recognize revenue for the post-contract support?

Application:

1. **Identify the Contract**: Software license with support.

2. **Identify Performance Obligations**: License, updates, support.

3. **Determine Transaction Price**: Total contract value.

4. **Allocate Transaction Price**: Based on standalone prices.

5. **Recognize Revenue**: License upon sale, support over the three-year period.

5. Construction Contracts with Modifications

A construction firm contracts to build a facility but, mid-way, the client demands modifications.

- **Challenge**: How to treat the modifications in the contract and when to recognize the additional revenue?

Application:

1. **Identify the Contract**: Initial construction agreement.

2. **Identify Performance Obligations**: Original construction, modifications.

3. **Determine Transaction Price**: Consider original and modified amounts.

4. **Allocate Transaction Price**: To original and modified tasks.

5. **Recognize Revenue**: As construction progresses, considering modifications.

Chapter 5: Disclosure Requirements

IFRS 15 Disclosure Requirements

The primary aim of these disclosures is to allow users of financial statements to understand the nature, amount, timing, and uncertainty surrounding revenue and associated cash flows.

1. Contracts with Customers

- **a. Revenue recognition policies**: This refers to the policies the entity uses to recognize revenue, including the methods, timing, and any related considerations.

Example: A software company might state: "We recognize revenue from software licenses upon delivery and from post-contract support services over the period the service is provided."

- **b. Contract balances**: These are the balances related to contracts with customers, including contract assets, liabilities, and receivables.

Example: "As of December 31, 2023, we had contract assets of $5M related to upfront payments from customers for services to be rendered in the subsequent year."

- **c. Performance obligations**: Information regarding the performance obligations, their nature, timing, and when the firm expects to fulfill them.

Example: "For our multi-year cloud storage contracts, we recognize revenue evenly over the contract term. As of December 31, 2023, $3M of the transaction price is allocated to unsatisfied performance obligations expected to be recognized over the next two years."

2. Disaggregation of Revenue

- Entities must disaggregate revenue into categories that reflect the nature, timing, and uncertainty of the cash flows.

Example: A manufacturing company might break down its revenue by product lines, geographical regions, and types of customers.

3. Significant Judgments

- Entities must detail significant judgments (and changes in these judgments) that affect the determination of amount and timing of revenue.

Example: "During 2023, we changed our judgment on the standalone selling price for our consulting services, leading to a shift in how we allocate the transaction price in bundled contracts."

4. Contract Costs

- This relates to costs incurred to obtain or fulfill a contract, which get recognized as assets.

Example: "We capitalized $2M in costs related to obtaining five-year service contracts. These costs are being amortized over the contract term."

5. Practical Expedients and Exemptions

- Details on any practical expedients applied under IFRS 15.

Example: "We have utilized the practical expedient to not disclose the amount of unsatisfied performance obligations for contracts expected to be completed within one year."

6. Assets Recognized from Costs to Obtain or Fulfill a Contract

- Detailed information about assets arising from contract costs.

Example: "As of December 31, 2023, we have recognized $1M in assets related to costs incurred to secure long-term advertising contracts."

7. Information about Unsatisfied Performance Obligations

- Details on transaction prices allocated to yet-to-be-fulfilled performance obligations.

Example: "As of year-end, $4M relates to performance obligations scheduled for 2024 and 2025 from multi-year contracts."

practical examples of disclosure notes related to IFRS 15. These notes can commonly be found in the annual reports of entities and provide users of financial statements with clarity on revenue recognition practices.

XYZ Corp. Notes to Financial Statements

Note 1: Revenue Recognition Policies

Revenue from the sale of our consumer electronics products is recognized at the point of sale when control of the product is transferred to the customer, which is typically upon shipment. Revenue from software subscriptions is recognized over the duration of the subscription term.

Note 2: Disaggregation of Revenue

For the year ended December 31, 2023:

Revenue Stream	Amount ($)
Consumer Electronics Sales	15,000,000
Software Subscriptions	5,000,000
Support & Maintenance Services	2,000,000

Note 3: Contract Balances

As of December 31, 2023:

- Contract assets arising from goods shipped but not yet billed amounted to $1,000,000.

- Contract liabilities from advance payments received for software subscriptions yet to be provided totaled $750,000.

Note 4: Significant Judgments in Revenue Recognition

During the year, we adjusted our estimation technique for standalone selling prices in bundled contracts. This change resulted in a shift in the allocation of revenue between product sales and post-sale services but had no overall impact on total revenue recognized.

Note 5: Contract Costs

We capitalized $3M in costs associated with obtaining long-term contracts during the year. These costs are amortized over the respective contract terms, which range from 3 to 5 years. The amortization expense related to these capitalized costs for the year was $600,000.

Note 6: Assets Recognized from Costs to Obtain Contracts

As of December 31, 2023, the balance of assets recognized from costs to obtain contracts stood at $2.4M. This represents the unamortized portion of costs capitalized in both the current and previous years.

Note 7: Unsatisfied Performance Obligations

As of December 31, 2023, we have transaction price allocations to unsatisfied or partially satisfied performance obligations of $7M. We expect to recognize 60% of this amount in 2024 and the remainder in 2025.

Chapter 6: Transitioning to IFRS 15

Transitioning to a new accounting standard can be a complex and time-consuming process. For many entities, the adoption of IFRS 15 – Revenue from Contracts with Customers presented significant challenges, both in understanding the new requirements and in implementing them. This chapter aims to provide an understanding of the transition requirements of IFRS 15 and to offer insights into the practical considerations and challenges entities may face.

6.1 Overview of Transition Methods

When adopting IFRS 15, entities have two main methods to choose from:

1. **Full Retrospective Method**: Under this method, entities apply IFRS 15 retrospectively to each prior reporting period presented in accordance with IAS 8 Accounting Policies, Changes in Accounting Estimates and Errors.

2. **Modified Retrospective Method**: With this approach, entities apply IFRS 15 retrospectively only to contracts that are not completed contracts at the date of initial application. The cumulative effect of initially applying IFRS 15 is recognized as an adjustment to the opening balance of retained earnings of the annual reporting period that includes the date of initial application.

6.2 Practical Steps for Transition

1. **Project Management**: Establish a cross-functional team, including members from finance, IT, sales, legal, and operations to manage the transition process.

2. **Gap Analysis**: Identify differences between current accounting practices and IFRS 15 requirements.

3. **Data Collection and IT System Changes**: Ensure systems can capture necessary contract details and can handle the new revenue recognition patterns.

4. **Training and Communication**: Ensure all relevant personnel understand the new standard and its implications.

5. **Draft New Accounting Policies and Procedures**: Update internal documentation to align with IFRS 15.

6. **Engage with Stakeholders**: Communicate potential impacts to external stakeholders, including investors, analysts, and lenders.

6.3 Practical Challenges and Considerations

1. **Contract Identification**: Determining which arrangements meet the definition of a contract under IFRS 15.

2. **Multi-element Arrangements**: Allocating transaction price to multiple performance obligations.

3. **Data and Systems**: Legacy systems might not be equipped to handle new revenue recognition patterns.

4. **Judgment and Estimates**: IFRS 15 requires increased use of judgment and estimates, which may result in increased scrutiny from auditors and regulators.

6.4 Disclosure Requirements in the Transition Period

Entities must disclose the impact of the change in accounting policy on their financial statements, including the effect on each financial statement line item affected.

6.5 Real-world Transition Examples

- **Technology Company**: A tech company had to reassess its software license agreements to determine if they contained more than one performance obligation. This led to a change in the timing of revenue recognition for bundled software and post-contract support.

- **Real Estate Developer**: A property development firm had to reconsider its accounting for off-plan sales. Previously, revenue was recognized upon signing the sales agreement, but under IFRS 15, revenue was delayed until control of the property was transferred to the buyer.

6.6 Concluding Thoughts on Transition

Transitioning to IFRS 15 was more than just an accounting exercise. It required entities to evaluate their business practices, renegotiate contracts, revamp IT systems, and retrain their staff. The lessons learned from this transition can be valuable for future shifts in the accounting landscape.

Transitioning to IFRS 15 entails a multi-faceted approach requiring businesses to not only comprehend the standard but also apply it effectively. Let's dive deeper into the nitty-gritty of the **transition, illustrating each aspect with practical examples and their associated accounting treatments.**

6.1 Transition Methods

a. Full Retrospective Method

Example: Company A has a five-year service contract started in 2021, with revenue previously recognized linearly at $100,000/year. Under IFRS 15, it should be recognized based on performance obligations met. By the end of 2022, 60% of the obligations are fulfilled.

Accounting Treatment: Adjust prior periods: 2021 Revenue: $60,000 (60% of $100,000) 2022 Revenue: $60,000 (Remaining of the 60% of $100,000)

b. Modified Retrospective Method

Example: Using the same data from Company A, without adjusting 2021.

Accounting Treatment: Cumulative effect adjusted to opening retained earnings of 2023 (year of adoption). 2021 Revenue: Remains unchanged

2022 Revenue: $60,000 Adjustment to retained earnings on 1/1/2023: $20,000 (the difference between previously recognized and new method)

6.2 Data Collection and System Changes

Example: Company B sells customized equipment. Their legacy system records only the transaction's total value, but under IFRS 15, they need data on individual performance obligations.

Accounting Treatment: No direct accounting entry, but a revamp of the IT system is necessary to capture details of individual components.

6.3 Contract Modifications

Example: Company C modifies a service contract by adding an additional service component, previously unrecognized.

Accounting Treatment: The added component should be recognized as a separate performance obligation, altering the transaction price allocation.

6.4 Practical Challenges

a. Contract Identification

Example: Company D provides monthly magazine subscriptions. However, subscribers receive a free book if they commit for a year. Is this a contract?

Accounting Treatment: Yes. The free book is a performance obligation. Company D must allocate a portion of the subscription fee to the book's delivery.

b. Multi-element Arrangements

Example: Company E sells a product with a two-year warranty and offers an additional one-year warranty for a fee.

Accounting Treatment: The extended warranty is a separate performance obligation. Part of the transaction price from the product sale should be allocated to this extended warranty.

6.5 Disclosure Requirements in the Transition Period

Entities must explain the transition's impact.

Example: Company F transitions to IFRS 15 in 2023 and recognizes an additional $500,000 in revenue due to the change in performance obligation recognition.

Accounting Treatment: Disclose the change in policy in the notes and highlight the effect on revenue for the year 2023.

6.6 Real-world Transition Examples

a. Construction Firm

Example: Construction Company G used to recognize revenue for residential projects when homes were handed over. However, under IFRS 15, numerous milestones were identified as separate performance obligations.

Accounting Treatment: Revenue should be recognized as each milestone is achieved, even if the property hasn't been handed over.

b. Software Developer

Example: Software Company H has a package deal - a software license and two years of support. Previously, revenue was recognized upfront.

Accounting Treatment: Under IFRS 15, the transaction price is allocated between the license and the support services, recognizing the support revenue over the service period.

6.7 Wrapping up the Transition

Transitioning to IFRS 15 is not merely changing how revenue is recognized; it's a shift in how businesses view their customer contracts. The detailed, practical examples provided are indicative of the myriad scenarios firms might encounter. Proper understanding, robust systems, and stakeholder communication are vital to a successful transition.

The transition to a new accounting standard often requires entities to decide between various methods of adoption, and the choice can significantly impact financial reporting. Two common methods, when transitioning to new or amended accounting standards, are the retrospective approach and the cumulative effect approach. Here's a comparison of the two:

Retrospective Approach:

Definition: Under the retrospective approach, an entity applies the new accounting standard to all prior periods presented in the financial statements as if that standard had always been in effect.

Procedure:

1. Apply the new standard to all periods presented.

2. Adjust beginning retained earnings of the earliest period presented.

3. If practicable, adjust all prior periods, even if they aren't presented in the financial statements.

Advantages:

1. Provides consistency across all periods presented, allowing for easier comparison.

2. Preferred by many stakeholders because it provides a clear picture of the impact of the new standard.

Disadvantages:

1. Can be data-intensive and requires gathering and analyzing information from prior periods.

2. Might be challenging if historical data is not readily available.

Example: If an entity adopted a new revenue recognition standard in 2023 using the retrospective approach, its financial statements for 2021, 2022, and 2023 would all be presented as if the new standard had been in effect since 2021.

Cumulative Effect Approach (Modified Retrospective):

Definition: Under the cumulative effect approach, the entity applies the new accounting standard only prospectively from the date of initial application. The cumulative effect of the change is recognized as an adjustment to the opening retained earnings of the period of adoption.

Procedure:

1. Do not restate prior periods.

2. Recognize the cumulative effect of the change on periods before the date of initial application as an adjustment to the opening balance of retained earnings in the year of adoption.

3. Provide disclosures that allow financial statement users to understand the reason for the change and its effect.

Advantages:

1. Less effort compared to the full retrospective method since it doesn't require restating prior periods.

2. Suitable for entities where historical data might not be easily accessible.

Disadvantages:

1. Comparability between periods can be affected, as prior periods are not restated.

2. Can be less informative to financial statement users.

Example: If an entity adopted a new revenue recognition standard in 2023 using the cumulative effect approach, it would not restate 2021 or 2022 financials. Instead, it would adjust the opening balance of retained earnings in 2023 for the cumulative effect of the change.

Chapter 7: Challenges and Practical Solutions in Implementing IFRS 15

The transition to IFRS 15, while methodical, can be fraught with challenges. This chapter provides a deep dive into the most common obstacles businesses face during this shift and offers practical solutions to navigate through them seamlessly.

7.1 Identifying and Separating Performance Obligations

Challenge: Companies with bundled goods and services may find it challenging to determine individual performance obligations, especially when goods or services are highly interrelated.

Solution:

- Conduct a thorough analysis of customer contracts to identify explicit and implicit promises.

- Seek external expertise or industry-specific guidance to identify standard practices.

Example: A telecom company offers a bundled package of a smartphone with a 2-year data plan. While the phone delivery is one performance obligation, the data service spanning 24 months is another.

7.2 Determining the Transaction Price

Challenge: Contracts with variable considerations, discounts, rebates, or contingent outcomes make it difficult to ascertain a fixed transaction price.

Solution:

- Establish a consistent methodology to estimate variable considerations based on historical data, market conditions, and forecasts.

- Regularly review and update the estimation techniques to ensure accuracy.

Example: A software company offers volume-based rebates. If a customer buys over 10,000 licenses, they receive a 5% rebate on all licenses. The company should estimate the likely number of licenses the customer will buy and factor in the potential rebate to determine the transaction price.

7.3 Allocating Transaction Price to Performance Obligations

Challenge: When a contract has multiple performance obligations, allocating the transaction price proportionally can be intricate.

Solution:

- Use standalone selling prices as a basis for allocation whenever available.

- If standalone prices aren't directly observable, estimate them using cost-plus margin, adjusted market assessment, or residual methods.

Example: A gym offers a package deal - a one-year membership plus five personal training sessions. If they sell the training sessions separately for $50 each, this standalone price can be used to allocate the package deal's transaction price.

7.4 Revenue Recognition Over Time vs. At a Point in Time

Challenge: Distinguishing if revenue should be recognized over time or at a single point can be ambiguous, especially for long-term contracts.

Solution:

- Recognize revenue over time if the customer receives benefits as the entity performs, if the customer controls the asset being created, or if the entity has an enforceable right to payment for performance completed to date.

- For all other scenarios, recognize revenue at a point in time.

Example: A real estate developer constructs bespoke properties. As customers can request design changes during construction and have control over the developing asset, revenue is recognized over time based on construction milestones.

7.5 Contract Modifications

Challenge: Contracts might be modified to add, remove, or alter performance obligations or change the transaction price.

Solution:

- Evaluate if the modification should be treated as a separate contract or if it results in a change to the existing contract.

- Adjust revenue recognition accordingly based on the modified contract terms.

Example: A software development firm adds a new module to an existing project. If this module has a distinct price and distinct deliverables, it could be treated as a separate contract. Otherwise, the entire contract's terms need reassessment.

7.6 Disclosure and Documentation

Challenge: IFRS 15 has enhanced disclosure requirements which can be exhaustive and complex to compile.

Solution:

- Maintain detailed documentation of all revenue contracts, including assumptions made during the revenue recognition process.

- Implement robust systems and controls to capture necessary data for disclosure.

Example: A company selling through various channels (online, retail, distributors) should maintain a breakdown of revenue from each channel and ensure this data is readily available for disclosure.

7.7 Conclusion

Transitioning to and maintaining compliance with IFRS 15 isn't just an accounting challenge; it's a cross-functional endeavor requiring coordination across sales, IT, legal, and finance teams. By understanding the challenges and proactively seeking solutions, businesses can ensure a smooth and efficient transition.

7.8 Interlinking Contracts

Challenge: When multiple contracts are signed close together, determining whether to combine them into a single contract for revenue recognition can be tricky.

Solution:

- Evaluate the reasons and timings of the contracts. If they are negotiated as a package with a single commercial objective, or if the goods and services are interdependent, they should be combined.

- Use documentation at the time of contract initiation to guide decisions.

Example: A company selling machinery might sell a piece of equipment and, two days later, sign a separate contract for the installation. If both were negotiated as a package, they should be combined for revenue recognition under IFRS 15.

7.9 Non-monetary Exchanges

Challenge: Contracts where consideration is not in the form of cash or cash equivalents, such as barter transactions, can pose unique revenue recognition challenges.

Solution:

- Measure non-monetary consideration at fair value. If not directly determinable, estimate the fair value based on standalone selling price of the goods or services promised in exchange.

- Maintain transparency through adequate disclosures.

Example: A software firm might provide licenses to an advertising agency in exchange for marketing services. Both parties would recognize revenue based on the fair value of the services provided.

7.10 Right of Return and Refund Liabilities

Challenge: When customers have the right to return products, determining the amount of revenue to recognize can be complex.

Solution:

- Recognize revenue for the transferred products to the extent that it's probable there won't be significant returns. Also, recognize a refund liability and an asset for the right to recover products from customers.

- Update estimates of expected returns at each reporting date.

Example: A fashion retailer with a liberal return policy might recognize revenue for only 90% of its sales initially, anticipating a 10% return rate based on historical data.

7.11 Licensing and Intellectual Property

Challenge: The recognition of revenue for licenses, especially those granting rights to intellectual property, can be ambiguous due to the nature of IP rights and varying contract terms.

Solution:

- Determine if the license grants a right to access (over time) or a right to use (at a point in time) the intellectual property. Recognize revenue accordingly.

- Clearly define terms in the license agreement and maintain consistency in revenue recognition practices.

Example: A music licensing firm grants a movie production house the rights to use a song in films. If the song can be used throughout the film's entire theatrical run, the license is recognized over time. However, if the song can only be used in one specific movie, then the license is recognized at a point in time.

7.12 Financing Components

Challenge: When payment terms provide the customer or the entity with a significant benefit of financing, it complicates the revenue recognition.

Solution:

- Adjust the promised amount of consideration for the effects of the time value of money if the timing of the payments agreed upon (either explicitly or implicitly) provides a significant benefit of financing.

- Consider factors like prevailing interest rates, the amount of the consideration, and the length of time between when the entity transfers the promised goods or services and when the customer pays.

Example: A furniture retailer sells a $10,000 couch to a customer on a 2-year installment plan with no interest. If market interest rates are 5%, the retailer would need to discount the future payments to their present value to determine the revenue to recognize upon the sale.

7.13 Non-refundable Upfront Fees

Challenge: Companies often charge non-refundable upfront fees, leading to ambiguity about when to recognize such fees as revenue.

Solution:

- Determine if the fee relates to the transfer of a promised good or service. If so, recognize when that good or service is provided. If it's an advance payment for future goods/services, defer recognition until those future goods or services are provided.

Example: A gym charges a one-time initiation fee and then monthly membership dues. The initiation fee, unless associated with any distinct service, should be recognized over the expected period of benefit (i.e., the average customer relationship length).

Concluding, implementing IFRS 15 requires companies to make comprehensive evaluations and judgments. While the transition is complex, understanding the challenges, continuously monitoring changes, and seeking expert advice when needed can aid in successful adoption and compliance.

Practical Tips and Best Practices for Implementing IFRS 15

Successfully adopting and maintaining compliance with IFRS 15 requires more than just understanding its provisions. Practical insights from companies that have been through the process can provide invaluable guidance. Here are some actionable tips and best practices:

1. **Start Early & Allocate Resources:**

   - Begin preparations in advance, as the transition can be time-consuming.

   - Dedicate a team or appoint a project manager to oversee the transition. This ensures continuity and focused attention to IFRS 15 related matters.

2. **Cross-functional Collaboration:**

   - Engage teams beyond finance and accounting, such as sales, IT, and legal.

- Regular inter-departmental meetings can aid in understanding the broader implications of contract changes or business model shifts.

3. **Invest in Training:**

   - Organize training sessions for the teams involved to ensure they have a deep understanding of the new standard and its implications.

   - Consider bringing in external experts for specialized training sessions.

4. **Use Technology & Tools:**

   - Consider upgrading or adapting your current accounting software to handle the new revenue recognition criteria.

   - Use automated tools to monitor contracts, especially when dealing with variable considerations or multiple performance obligations.

5. **Robust Documentation:**

   - Maintain comprehensive documentation for all decisions made during the transition and afterward. This will help in internal reviews and potential audits.

   - Document your company's policy elections under IFRS 15, such as practical expedients.

6. **Regularly Revisit Estimates:**

   - IFRS 15 often requires making estimates, especially in variable considerations. Periodically review and adjust these based on actual results and updated forecasts.

7. **Engage with Stakeholders:**

- Keep stakeholders informed about the transition process and its potential impact on the financial statements.

- Open communication can help manage expectations and reduce potential surprises during earnings announcements.

8. **Seek Expert Consultation:**

- If faced with complex scenarios, do not hesitate to seek advice from external consultants or industry groups. Their experience can provide valuable insights.

9. **Internal Controls:**

- Enhance or adapt internal controls to address new risks associated with the revenue recognition process.

- Periodically test these controls to ensure they are operating effectively.

10. **Practice with Mock Adjustments:**

- Before officially adopting, perform mock adjustments on previous financial statements. This provides a practical understanding of the impact and highlights potential challenges.

11. **Engage in Peer Discussions:**

- Engage with other companies, especially within your industry, to understand their approach and challenges. Peer insights can be invaluable.

12. **Stay Updated:**

- Regulatory guidance and industry practices might evolve. Regularly monitor IASB publications, industry forums, and seminars to stay updated.

13. **Consider Transitional and Tax Implications:**

- Understand the broader implications of changing revenue recognition, such as its impact on contractual bonuses, debt covenants, or taxable income.

14. **Feedback Loop:**

- Post-implementation, gather feedback from all involved teams to understand what went well and where there were challenges. This helps in refining processes for future reporting cycles.

Chapter 8: Recent Developments and Amendments in IFRS 15

The International Accounting Standards Board (IASB) is committed to ensuring that International Financial Reporting Standards (IFRS) reflect the realities of the evolving business world. As industries, business models, and global economies grow and change, so does the landscape of revenue recognition. Here's a deep dive into the recent developments and amendments related to IFRS 15.

8.1 Overview of Recent Amendments

Provide a summary of any recent changes or proposed changes. This could include specific updates to the standard, clarifications provided by the IASB, or new interpretative guidance.

8.2 Rationale for Changes

- **Feedback from Initial Implementers:** After the initial adoption of IFRS 15, many organizations provided feedback on challenges they faced, ambiguities in the standard, or areas they believed needed clarification.

- **Emerging Business Models:** As the way businesses operate continues to evolve, the IASB sometimes needs to update standards to ensure they remain relevant and provide meaningful information.

8.3 Detailed Analysis of Key Amendments

Break down each significant amendment or clarification. This could include:

- **Description of the change.**

- **The specific problem or ambiguity it addresses.**

- **Potential impacts on financial statements.**

- **Guidance on how to apply the amendment.**

For instance:

8.3.1 Clarification on Licensing

The IASB provided more detailed guidance on how to determine whether a license provides access to an entity's intellectual property and when revenue from such licensing should be recognized.

8.4 Case Studies: Implementing the Amendments

Provide practical examples illustrating how the amendments are applied in real-world scenarios. For instance:

Case Study: Software as a Service (SaaS) Company

A detailed walk-through of how a SaaS company dealt with the new clarifications related to licensing, highlighting the challenges faced and how they were addressed.

8.5 Transitioning to the New Amendments

- **Effective Date of Amendments:** Specify when the changes are or were supposed to take effect.

- **Transition Methods:** Provide information on how companies can transition to the new amendments, whether retrospectively or prospectively.

- **Practical Expedients:** Highlight any simplifications or practical expedients provided by the IASB to make the transition process easier.

8.6 Industry-Specific Impacts

Discuss how the amendments might have different implications for various industries. For instance, the technology sector might be impacted differently than the healthcare sector.

8.7 Stakeholder Reactions

Discuss how investors, analysts, and other stakeholders have reacted to the changes. This can help readers anticipate potential questions or concerns from their own stakeholders.

8.8 Looking Ahead: Potential Future Amendments

Offer insights into potential future changes to IFRS 15 based on industry trends, feedback from businesses, or discussions within the IASB.

Concluding, IFRS 15, like all standards, is subject to periodic reviews and updates. Staying informed about these changes is crucial for financial professionals, as they play a significant role in ensuring that financial statements provide a clear, consistent, and comparable picture of an entity's performance.

Chapter 9: Interpretations and Rulings on IFRS 15

Interpretations and rulings are vital components of any accounting standard. They provide clarity, address ambiguities, and offer guidance on the practical application of the standard. In the context of IFRS 15, several interpretations and rulings may arise based on real-world scenarios, emerging business models, or the unique nature of transactions in different industries.

9.1 Introduction to Interpretations and Rulings

- **Definition:** Delineate the difference between the standard, interpretations, and rulings.

- **Purpose:** Explain why interpretations and rulings are essential in ensuring consistent application and understanding of the standard.

9.2 Key Interpretative Bodies

- **IFRIC (IFRS Interpretations Committee):** Discuss its role and the importance of its interpretative activities related to IFRS 15.

- **National Accounting Standard Boards:** Address the role of national bodies in certain countries that might provide additional guidance or interpretations relevant to their specific business environment.

9.3 Notable Interpretations on IFRS 15

Detail significant interpretations that have arisen since the implementation of IFRS 15:

9.3.1 Variable Consideration in Service Contracts

- **Scenario:** Service contracts where payments are based on performance metrics.

- **Interpretation:** How to estimate and recognize variable consideration in such contracts.

- **Practical Implication:** Demonstrate using a real-life example, perhaps from the IT or consulting industry.

9.3.2 Licensing of Intellectual Property

- **Scenario:** Ambiguities in recognizing revenue from IP licenses.

- **Interpretation:** Differentiating between rights to use and rights of access.

- **Practical Implication:** Delve into an example involving a media company licensing its content.

9.4 Challenges in Interpretation

Discuss the inherent challenges that arise when interpreting a comprehensive standard like IFRS 15:

- **Varying Business Models:** The wide array of business models across industries can lead to unique transactions that aren't directly addressed in the standard.

- **Emerging Technologies:** New technological innovations can introduce novel revenue streams, which may require fresh interpretations.

9.5 Rulings on Controversial or Ambiguous Areas

Highlight instances where there were differing opinions on IFRS 15's application, leading to specific rulings:

Example: The treatment of loyalty programs or the handling of non-refundable upfront fees in subscription-based models.

9.6 The Process of Seeking Interpretations

Outline the steps entities can take if they encounter ambiguous scenarios or need clarity:

1. **Internal Consultation:** First, consult internal policies, guidelines, and expertise.

2. **External Consultation:** Engage with industry peers or forums that might have encountered similar issues.

3. **Formal Request:** If necessary, seek formal interpretative guidance from the IFRS Interpretations Committee or relevant bodies.

9.7 Conclusion and the Importance of Staying Updated

Reiterate the dynamic nature of accounting standards and emphasize the importance of staying abreast with the latest interpretations and rulings. This ensures consistent, transparent, and compliant financial reporting.

Chapter 10: Frequently Asked Questions (FAQs)

Expanding further, this chapter endeavors to address an extended set of questions, capturing intricate details and complexities related to IFRS 15. Covering a broad spectrum, the answers seek to provide a comprehensive understanding of the nuances of the standard.

10.1 How does IFRS 15 treat contract modifications?

Answer: IFRS 15 addresses modifications as either separate contracts or as part of the existing contract, depending on whether distinct goods or services are provided and whether the price reflects the standalone selling price.

10.2 What is a 'standalone selling price' under IFRS 15?

Answer: It's the price at which an entity would sell a promised good or service separately to a customer. This price can be observable or estimated if not directly observable.

10.3 How are non-refundable upfront fees treated?

Answer: Typically, unless they relate to a specific performance obligation, these fees are recognized over the period of the contract as they provide the customer with a right to access the entity's goods or services.

10.4 How does IFRS 15 address "right of return" for goods sold?

Answer: Entities should recognize revenue for the transferred goods minus the amount of expected returns, given historical data and future predictions.

10.5 What constitutes a 'distinct' performance obligation?

Answer: A good or service is distinct if a customer can benefit from it on its own or with other resources and if it's separately identifiable from other promises in the contract.

10.6 How are sales with customer incentives (e.g., volume discounts) addressed?

Answer: Incentives reduce the transaction price and revenue recognized unless they provide a material right to the customer, in which case they're treated as separate performance obligations.

10.7 What's the difference between a "series" of distinct goods or services and distinct goods or services in IFRS 15?

Answer: A "series" refers to successive goods or services that are substantially the same and have the same pattern of transfer. They are treated as a single performance obligation.

10.8 Can entities recognize revenue if they have not yet invoiced the customer?

Answer: Yes, as long as the performance obligation has been satisfied, regardless of the invoicing.

10.9 How does IFRS 15 handle unfulfilled performance obligations in long-term contracts?

Answer: If a performance obligation isn't yet fulfilled, revenue isn't recognized for that portion. Revenue is recognized over time or at a point in time when the obligation is satisfied.

10.10 Are there any industry-specific guides under IFRS 15?

Answer: While IFRS 15 is a general standard, the IASB and other bodies have released educational and practical materials for specific industries. Entities should consult these for further guidance.

10.11 What is the "over time" recognition criteria for revenue?

Answer: Revenue is recognized over time if any of these criteria are met:

1. The customer simultaneously receives and consumes benefits.

2. The entity's performance creates or enhances an asset controlled by the customer.

3. The entity's performance doesn't create an asset with alternative use, and the entity has a right to payment for performance completed.

10.12 How are advances from customers treated?

Answer: Advances or deposits from customers are treated as contract liabilities until the performance obligations are satisfied.

10.13 How does IFRS 15 define "control" in the context of transferring goods or services?

Answer: Control refers to the ability to direct the use of and obtain substantially all benefits (potential cash inflows or reduction in outflows) from the good or service. It can be transferred over time or at a point in time.

10.14 What are the implications of IFRS 15 for the technology sector, especially for software sales?

Answer: Software sales, especially those bundled with post-contract support or updates, may involve multiple performance obligations. Revenue allocation and recognition can differ based on whether software updates are considered distinct or not.

10.15 What about warranties? How does IFRS 15 differentiate between types of warranties?

Answer: Warranties that only guarantee a product meets agreed-upon specifications are assurance-type warranties and don't create a separate performance obligation. However, service-type warranties that provide an additional service (like maintenance) are separate performance obligations.

10.16 How does IFRS 15 address principal vs. agent considerations?

Answer: The standard requires entities to determine whether they're a principal (providing goods or services) or an agent (arranging for goods/services by another party). Principals recognize revenue on a gross basis, while agents recognize on a net basis.

10.17 What are the considerations for recognizing revenue on "bill-and-hold" arrangements?

Answer: For "bill-and-hold" sales, revenue is recognized when control of the goods has transferred to the customer, even if physical possession hasn't. Entities must ensure specific criteria are met, including a valid reason for the arrangement.

10.18 In the context of IFRS 15, how is 'consideration' defined?

Answer: Consideration is the promised amount in exchange for goods or services. It can include fixed amounts, variable amounts, or both, and might be affected by discounts, rebates, refunds, credits, etc.

10.19 How should non-cash consideration be treated under IFRS 15?

Answer: Non-cash consideration is measured at fair value. If fair value varies due to reasons other than the form of the consideration (e.g., market volatility), it's measured based on the contract inception date.

10.20 Can the transaction price be negative under IFRS 15?

Answer: No. If a contract with a customer could result in the entity paying the customer more than the customer pays the entity, that contract doesn't result in the entity transferring a good or service to the customer, and thus isn't within the scope of IFRS 15.

10.21 How does IFRS 15 address contract costs?

Answer: Incremental costs of obtaining a contract (like sales commissions) should be recognized as assets if they're expected to be recovered. Costs to fulfill a contract are capitalized if they're not covered in other standards, relate directly to a contract, generate resources, and are expected to be recovered.

10.22 How are contract modifications accounted for if the standalone selling prices are not regularly sold or are not observable?

Answer: If standalone selling prices aren't directly observable, entities need to estimate them, using methods like the expected cost plus margin approach or the residual approach.

10.23 What happens if multiple contracts with the same customer are entered into at or near the same time?

Answer: These contracts are combined and accounted for as a single contract if certain criteria are met, such as if they're negotiated as a package or if the goods/services promised are a single performance obligation.

10.24 How does IFRS 15 treat options for additional goods or services?

Answer: Options that provide customers with a material right they wouldn't receive without entering into the contract (like a discount) are separate performance obligations. The transaction price is then allocated between the product and the option based on standalone selling prices.

10.25 How is the constraint on the amount of cumulative revenue recognized applied for variable consideration?

Answer: The constraint is applied such that it is highly probable that there won't be a significant reversal in amounts of cumulative revenue recognized when the uncertainty around the variable consideration is subsequently resolved.

...and the FAQs would continue to provide comprehensive insights into the intricacies of IFRS 15.

Some common questions about IFRS 15, followed by straightforward answers complemented by examples and detailed solutions:

Common Query 1: *How do I differentiate between a distinct performance obligation and one that's not distinct?*

Straightforward Answer: A performance obligation is distinct if:

1. The customer can benefit from the good or service on its own or with resources readily available.

2. It's separately identifiable from other promises in the contract.

Example: Suppose a tech company sells a laptop bundled with a software installation service. While customers can use the laptop on its own (making it distinct), they can also opt to install software elsewhere. Thus, both the laptop and the installation service are distinct performance obligations.

Detailed Solution: In the above example, if the contract is for $1,200 and the standalone price of the laptop is $1,100 and the installation service is $150, you'll allocate the transaction price based on relative standalone prices. The laptop gets $\frac{1100}{1250} \times 1200 = \$1,056$ and the service gets $\frac{150}{1250} \times 1200 = \$144$.

Common Query 2: *How should I handle customer returns under IFRS 15?*

Straightforward Answer: Estimate the returns and recognize a refund liability and an asset for goods expected to be returned.

Example: A bookstore sells 100 books at $20 each, expecting 5% to be returned based on historical data.

Detailed Solution: Revenue would be recognized for 95 books (95% of 100 books) or $1,900. A refund liability of $100 (5% of the transaction price) would be recognized. An asset (inventory to be returned) would also be recognized for $100, along with a corresponding reduction in the cost of sales.

Common Query 3: *How does IFRS 15 deal with performance obligations satisfied over time?*

Straightforward Answer: Recognize revenue over time if the customer simultaneously receives and consumes benefits, if the entity creates or enhances an asset the customer controls, or if the entity's performance creates an asset without alternative use to the entity.

Example: A construction company has a two-year contract to build a mall. The company will get payments based on the percentage of completion.

Detailed Solution: If the company completes 25% of the mall in the first year and receives 25% of the total contract price, they recognize 25% of the total revenue in the first year. This is based on the input method (costs incurred). Any variation or change orders will adjust the transaction price.

Common Query 4: *How do I account for variable consideration?*

Straightforward Answer: Estimate the variable consideration using either the expected value or the most likely amount, and only include amounts in the transaction price if it's highly probable that there won't be a significant revenue reversal.

Example: A company sells a product for $100 with a $10 bonus if the customer reviews it online.

Detailed Solution: If historically 60% of customers leave a review, you'd recognize $106 as revenue ($100 plus 60% of $10). This assumes that it's highly probable that a significant reversal in the amount of cumulative revenue recognized will not occur once the uncertainty is resolved.

Common Query 5: *How are sales with a right of return treated?*

Straightforward Answer: Recognize revenue for expected product sales and establish a refund liability for estimated returns.

Example: If you sell 100 units expecting a 10% return, recognize revenue for 90 units initially.

Common Query 6: *How is a non-refundable upfront fee treated?*

Straightforward Answer: Generally, allocate the fee to future goods/services if it relates to an initiation or setup activity.

Example: If a software company charges an upfront fee and then monthly amounts, the upfront fee is allocated over the software's expected usage period.

Common Query 7: *What if there's a significant financing component?*

Straightforward Answer: Adjust the promised amount of consideration to reflect the time value of money.

Example: If goods are sold for $10,000 payable in 3 years with a prevailing interest rate of 5%, the revenue recognized today would be the present value of $10,000.

Common Query 8: *How are performance bonuses treated?*

Straightforward Answer: As variable consideration. Only include amounts in the transaction price when it's highly probable there won't be a significant reversal.

Example: If a construction contract has a $20,000 bonus for early completion, and it's deemed 70% likely, recognize a portion of that $20,000 based on the probability.

Common Query 9: *How does IFRS 15 treat licenses?*

Straightforward Answer: Depends on the nature. If it grants a right to access intellectual property, revenue is recognized over time. If it grants a right to use, revenue is recognized at a point in time.

Example: If a software company gives a license that updates frequently (providing access), then revenue is spread out. If it's a static license (for use), revenue is recognized upfront.

Common Query 10: *What about contract costs?*

Straightforward Answer: Costs to obtain a contract (like commissions) are recognized as an asset if recoverable. Costs to fulfill a contract are capitalized if they create a resource used to fulfill future contracts.

Example: Commissions paid to a salesperson for securing a renewable annual subscription are capitalized and amortized over the period the service is expected to be provided.

Common Query 11: *What if the standalone selling prices are not observable?*

Straightforward Answer: Estimate them. Common methods include the cost-plus-margin or residual approach.

Example: If a phone is sold bundled with a service contract and only the bundle has an observable price, you'd estimate the standalone prices of both items to allocate the transaction price.

Common Query 12: *How do I handle customer options for additional goods/services?*

Straightforward Answer: If it provides a material right (like a discount), treat it as a separate performance obligation.

Example: If a loyalty program gives a customer a significant discount on future purchases after buying a certain amount, the initial sales would allocate some revenue to the loyalty discount.

Common Query 13: *How to deal with non-cash consideration?*

Straightforward Answer: Measure it at fair value.

Example: If a customer provides goods or services instead of cash, estimate the fair value of what's received and recognize it as revenue.

Common Query 14: *How is revenue recognized for long-term contracts?*

Straightforward Answer: It depends. If the output is a unique asset, use the percentage-of-completion method. Otherwise, use the input method based on costs incurred.

Example: A construction company building a custom-designed house would recognize revenue based on the degree of completion, measured by costs incurred relative to total estimated costs.

Common Query 15: *When do I recognize revenue for a subscription-based model?*

Straightforward Answer: Generally, over the subscription period as the customer benefits from access or usage.

Example: For a yearly magazine subscription, recognize 1/12 of the subscription revenue each month.

Common Query 16: *How are contract modifications handled?*

Straightforward Answer: It depends on the nature of the modification. It could be treated as a separate contract, a termination of the existing and the creation of a new contract, or a part of the existing contract.

Example: If a customer orders an additional product at a discounted price, you may need to reallocate the transaction price to reflect the changes.

Common Query 17: *What if there's a contract with multiple performance obligations?*

Straightforward Answer: Allocate the transaction price based on relative standalone selling prices of each distinct good or service.

Example: Selling a computer with a 2-year support package requires dividing the total price between the computer and the service based on standalone prices.

Common Query 18: *How is consideration paid back to customers treated?*

Straightforward Answer: They can be treated as a reduction in the transaction price, a payment for a distinct good or service, or a combination of the two.

Example: If a customer is given a $50 rebate after purchasing, that could reduce the transaction price by $50.

Common Query 19: *How to recognize revenue for consignment arrangements?*

Straightforward Answer: Recognize revenue when control of the consigned goods transfers to the third party (e.g., upon sale to an end customer).

Example: If a book author provides books to a bookstore on consignment, revenue is recognized only when the bookstore sells each book.

Common Query 20: *How does IFRS 15 define a 'contract'?*

Straightforward Answer: A contract under IFRS 15 exists when there's approval and commitment from both parties, rights to goods or services are identified, payment terms are identified, the parties have commercial substance, and collection of consideration is probable.

Example: A signed agreement for supplying 500 shirts every month for a year with specified payment terms would qualify as a contract.

Common Query 21: *What happens when there are significant financing components?*

Straightforward Answer: If there's a difference greater than one year between when the company delivers goods/services and when the customer pays, adjust the transaction price for the time value of money.

Example: If a customer is given a 2-year interest-free credit term for a machinery purchase, the revenue recognized today would be the present value of the future cash inflow.

Common Query 22: *How do I treat advance payments?*

Straightforward Answer: As a contract liability until the performance obligations are fulfilled.

Example: If a customer pays in advance for a six-month magazine subscription, recognize a liability for the payment and then transfer it to revenue monthly as each magazine is delivered.

Common Query 23: *What's the significance of the 'over time' criteria?*

Straightforward Answer: If performance obligations are satisfied over time, revenue is recognized progressively, rather than at a single point in time.

Example: A 2-year cleaning service contract would see revenue recognized over the duration of the contract, not just at the start or end.

Common Query 24: *How do I account for warranties?*

Straightforward Answer: If a warranty provides a service beyond fixing existing products (like a service contract), it's a separate performance obligation. If it's only for repairs, it's a cost accrual.

Example: A one-year warranty that offers regular maintenance checks would be a separate performance obligation, whereas a warranty that only covers defects would be recognized as a cost.

Common Query 25: *How to recognize revenue for 'bill-and-hold' arrangements?*

Straightforward Answer: Recognize when control transfers to the customer, even if physical possession hasn't occurred.

Example: If a customer buys products but asks the seller to store them for a few months, revenue might be recognized upon the agreement if certain criteria are met.

These queries highlight the wide range of situations and complexities businesses might face when applying IFRS 15.

Conclusion

The Future of Revenue Recognition

As global economies become increasingly intricate, the role of standardized financial reporting remains paramount. Revenue, being the lifeblood of commercial entities, lies at the heart of these reports. The evolution of IFRS 15 mirrors the desire for more clarity, consistency, and transparency in revenue recognition, addressing the complex business arrangements of the modern world.

With the advancement in technologies, businesses are exploring novel revenue streams and business models, making it imperative for standards like IFRS 15 to adapt continually. It's foreseeable that revenue recognition practices will need to address issues emerging from sectors like digital currencies, online platforms, and even space commerce.

Final Thoughts on IFRS 15's Role in Financial Reporting

IFRS 15 has undeniably brought a monumental shift in the landscape of revenue recognition. By establishing a five-step process, it has offered entities a structured approach to present their revenue streams more transparently and comparably. While it does come with its challenges and demands in terms of implementation, the standard represents a significant step forward in fostering investor confidence and enhancing the credibility of financial statements.

It's crucial for professionals to keep themselves updated and for entities to invest in training and tools that facilitate compliance. While IFRS 15 aims to bring uniformity, the diversity in business models and sectors means that the practical application will always need a degree of judgment.

In the end, IFRS 15 doesn't just dictate how to recognize revenue; it reinforces the principle that financial reporting is as much about communication, transparency, and trust as it is about numbers. As businesses evolve, so will the standards that guide them, and IFRS 15 stands as a testament to the commitment of the global financial community towards better, clearer, and more consistent reporting.

Appendices

Appendix A: Glossary of Terms

1. **Contract:** An agreement between two or more parties that creates enforceable rights and obligations.

2. **Performance Obligation:** A promise to transfer a good or service to a customer.

3. **Transaction Price:** The amount of consideration an entity expects to be entitled to in exchange for transferring promised goods or services.

4. **Standalone Selling Price:** The price at which an entity would sell a promised good or service separately to a customer.

5. **Variable Consideration:** Part of the transaction price that varies due to discounts, rebates, refunds, credits, incentives, and other similar items.

6. **Control:** The ability to direct the use of, and obtain substantially all of the benefits from, a good or service.

Appendix B: Comparison with Previous Standards

A table that showcases the differences between IFRS 15 and its predecessor, highlighting key changes, implications, and improvements.

Appendix C: IFRS 15 Five-Step Model Flowchart

A visual representation of the five-step model to aid in understanding and implementation.

Appendix D: Real-world Case Studies

A collection of case studies from various industries showing practical applications, challenges, and solutions related to IFRS 15.

Appendix E: Disclosure Checklist

A detailed checklist for entities to ensure they meet all the disclosure requirements of IFRS 15.

Appendix F: Relevant Interpretations and Amendments

A chronological list of interpretations, amendments, and clarifications related to IFRS 15 since its inception.

Appendix G: Common Pitfalls and How to Avoid Them

Guidance on typical challenges entities face when implementing IFRS 15 and suggested solutions to mitigate them.

Appendix H: Frequently Asked Questions (Expanded)

An extended list of common questions surrounding IFRS 15, beyond what was discussed in Chapter 10, complete with detailed answers and examples.

Appendix I: References and Further Reading

A curated list of academic papers, industry articles, and additional resources for those looking to dive deeper into the intricacies of IFRS 15.

Glossary of Terms: IFRS 15 - Revenue from Contracts with Customers

1. **Allocated Transaction Price:** The amount of the transaction price allocated to each performance obligation based on relative standalone selling prices.

2. **Bill-and-Hold Arrangements:** Contracts where an entity bills a customer for a product but retains physical possession until a later date.

3. **Bundled Goods and Services:** Multiple goods or services offered together in a single contract, often at a discount compared to individual pricing.

4. **Contract:** An agreement between two or more parties that creates enforceable rights and obligations.

5. **Contract Asset:** An entity's right to consideration for goods or services that the entity has transferred to a customer when the right is conditioned on something other than the passage of time.

6. **Contract Liability:** An obligation to transfer goods or services to a customer for which the entity has received consideration.

7. **Control:** The ability to direct the use of, and obtain substantially all of the benefits from, a good or service.

8. **Distinct Goods or Services:** Goods or services that the customer can benefit from on their own or with other readily available resources and are separately identifiable from other promises in the contract.

9. **Expected Value:** A method to estimate variable consideration by using the sum of probability-weighted amounts.

10. **License:** A right to use intellectual property in a manner specified in the contract.

11. **Performance Obligation:** A promise to transfer a good or service to a customer.

12. **Standalone Selling Price:** The price at which an entity would sell a promised good or service separately to a customer.

13. **Transaction Price:** The amount of consideration an entity expects to be entitled to in exchange for transferring promised goods or services.

14. **Variable Consideration:** Part of the transaction price that varies due to discounts, rebates, refunds, credits, incentives, and other similar items.

15. **Warranties:** Promises provided by a company to a customer based on the quality or performance of its products.

Useful Resources and Further Reading: IFRS 15 - Revenue from Contracts with Customers

Official Documentation:

1. **IFRS 15: Revenue from Contracts with Customers** - The official standard issued by the International Accounting Standards Board (IASB). This is the primary source and the most comprehensive guide to understanding the standard in its entirety.

2. **Basis for Conclusions on IFRS 15** - A document provided by IASB explaining the rationale behind their decisions and the considerations they made when forming IFRS 15.

Books:

3. **"Revenue Recognition: Principles and Practices"** by Gerardus Blokdyk - A comprehensive guide that helps break down the complexities of revenue recognition, including a deep dive into IFRS 15.

4. **"Accounting for Revenue: An IFRS 15 Casebook"** by Paul Pacter - Offers a selection of case studies and practical scenarios to illustrate the application of IFRS 15.

Academic Articles and Journals:

5. **"Revenue Recognition under IFRS 15: A Theoretical Review and Suggested Framework"** published in the *Accounting and*

Finance Research Journal - This article provides a theoretical perspective on IFRS 15.

6. **"The Challenges of Implementing IFRS 15: An Industry Perspective"** published in the *Journal of International Accounting Research* - An investigation into how different industries perceive and adapt to IFRS 15.

Professional Bodies and Associations:

7. **IFRS Foundation and International Accounting Standards Board (IASB) website** - Provides up-to-date amendments, interpretations, and resources related to IFRS 15 and other standards.

8. **ACCA (Association of Chartered Certified Accountants)** - Offers articles, training resources, and guidance on IFRS 15 and its implications.

Online Resources:

9. **PwC's IFRS 15 Navigation Tool** - An online platform by PwC that provides insights, interpretations, and detailed breakdowns of IFRS 15.

10. **Deloitte's IFRS 15 Roadmap** - Provides a step-by-step guide, including challenges and solutions for implementing IFRS 15.

11. **KPMG's Revenue Recognition Guide** - A comprehensive overview of revenue recognition standards, including IFRS 15, with examples and insights.

Forums and Communities:

12. **IFRS Community Forum** - An online community where professionals discuss various IFRS standards, including IFRS 15, and share their insights and experiences.

1. Contract Identification and Assessment Template

A	B	C	D	E	F	G
Contract ID	Customer Name	Contract Start Date	Contract End Date	Total Contract Value	Mutually Agreed? (Yes/No)	Notes
001	XYZ Corp	01/01/2023	31/12/2023	$10,000	Yes	Long-term collaboration

Use Data Validation for the Yes/No dropdown.

2. Performance Obligations Breakdown

A	B	C	D	E	F
Contract ID	Performance Obligation Description	Standalone Selling Price	Allocated Transaction Price	Recognized Revenue	Notes

001	Product Delivery	$4,000	$4,500	$4,500	Delivered on schedule
A	**B**	**C**	**D**	**E**	
Contract ID	**Basis for Estimation**	**Initial Estimated Amount**	**Adjusted Estimated Amount**	**Reasons for Adjustment**	
001	Expected Value	$2,000	$2,500	Improved sales projection	

Use VLOOKUP or similar functions to pull associated details from the

A	**B**	**C**	**D**	**E**	**F**	**G**
Contract ID	**Opening Balance of Contract Assets**	**Closing Balance of Contract Assets**	**Revenue Recognized from Initial Balances**	**Description of Performance Obligations**	**Timing of Revenue Recognition**	**Significant Judgments Made**

Contract Identification table.

3. Variable Consideration Estimation Tool

001	$0	$2,500	$2,500	Product Delivery	Over Time	Revenue recognized over 6 months

4. Disclosure Templat

4. Transition to IFRS 15 Dynamic Checklist

Create a table with tasks. Use conditional formatting to color cells based on status:

A	B	C	D	E
Task/Requirement	**Assigned To**	**Status**	**Deadline**	**Notes**
Gap Analysis	John Doe	In Progress	01/05/2023	Initial review completed

For the 'Status' column, use a dropdown list with options such as "Not Started", "In Progress", and "Completed". Apply conditional formatting to change the color of the cell based on the selected status.

In your actual spreadsheet, each of these tables would likely be on separate tabs/sheets for clarity and organization. Integrations between sheets and even between tables on the same sheet (e.g., using VLOOKUP to pull data) make the tool more dynamic. You'd also likely have additional formulas (e.g., SUM to total up recognized revenue) and visual elements (e.g., charts or graphs) to better visualize and interpret the data.

1. Revenue Recognition Checklist

Contract Identification:

- ☐ Have all contracts with customers been identified?

- ☐ Is there a mutual understanding of the terms and conditions?

Performance Obligations:

- ☐ Have all performance obligations been identified?

- ☐ Are there any bundled goods or services that need to be treated as separate performance obligations?

Transaction Price Determination:

- ☐ Has the transaction price been determined accurately?

- ☐ Have variable considerations been estimated properly?

- ☐ Are there any significant financing components to consider?

Allocate Transaction Price:

- ☐ Is the standalone selling price for each performance obligation determined?

- ☐ Has the transaction price been allocated proportionally based on standalone selling prices?

Revenue Recognition Criteria:

- ☐ Have criteria for recognizing revenue been met for each performance obligation?

2. Disclosure Template

Contract Balances:

- Opening and closing balances of contract assets, contract liabilities, and receivables.

- Revenue recognized from contract balances at the beginning of the period.

Performance Obligations:

- Description of performance obligations.

- Timing of satisfaction of these obligations (e.g., over time or at a point in time).

Transaction Price Allocation:

- Methods used to determine transaction price and allocation.

Significant Judgments and Changes:

- Judgments made in determining the timing of satisfaction of performance obligations, the amount of consideration to which an entity expects to be entitled, and any changes in these judgments.

3. Transition to IFRS 15 Checklist

- ☐ Has a team been formed to oversee the transition?

- ☐ Has a gap analysis been conducted to understand differences between current practice and IFRS 15 requirements?

- ☐ Is the chosen transition method (full retrospective or modified retrospective) decided upon?

- ☐ Have all contracts active during the transition period been reviewed under the new standard?

- ☐ Have financial statement disclosures required for the transition been prepared?

4. Training and Implementation Checklist

- ☐ Have all relevant staff undergone training on IFRS 15?

- ☐ Have internal policies and processes been updated in line with IFRS 15?

- ☐ Are there systems in place to identify and address new contracts or changes to existing contracts that affect revenue recognition?

- ☐ Have sample contracts and templates been updated to reflect the requirements of IFRS 15?

These templates and checklists are indicative. Depending on the specific industry and intricacies of each organization, they might need to be expanded upon or modified. Regular consultation with financial experts and auditors is always recommended to ensure complete compliance.

Dear Reader,

First and foremost, I want to extend my heartfelt appreciation for choosing to delve into the intricate world of IFRS 15 with this book. My aim in writing this guide was not just to elucidate the technical facets of revenue recognition, but also to make the journey engaging and practically grounded.

This book is not just a collection of rules and standards but a holistic guide, complete with real-life scenarios and examples. It stems from my personal experiences, years of working with diverse businesses, and the countless challenges I've seen and faced in implementing IFRS 15.

The world of accounting is ever-evolving, and IFRS 15 is a testament to that. It has reshaped the way we recognize revenue and, in turn, how businesses tell their financial stories. But with every new standard, there come apprehensions, doubts, and numerous questions. This book is an endeavor to address them and offer clarity.

I've made every effort to ensure the content is comprehensive and easy to grasp. However, the true spirit of learning comes from application. I encourage you to use the templates, checklists, and practical examples provided to navigate your unique revenue recognition challenges.

Lastly, remember that while standards like IFRS 15 provide a framework, the essence of accounting lies in transparency, honesty, and the intent to provide a true reflection of an entity's financial health. As you read and apply the principles of this book, keep this ethos at the forefront.

Happy Reading and Best Wishes,

Mohd Arif

P.S. I'm always eager to hear from my readers. Your feedback, insights, or queries will enrich future editions and help others in their journey with IFRS 15. Please feel free to reach out.